Neurodivergent Women

A Force to Be Reckoned With.

Louisa J. Gibso

A force to be reckoned with.

Disclaimers

This book is not a substitute for medical advice. The author is not a medical professional and does not claim to be able to diagnose or treat any medical conditions. If you have any concerns about your health, please consult a doctor or other qualified health care provider.

COPYRIGHT

Overview

Neurodivergent Women: A Force to Be Reckoned With is a captivating exploration of the unique strengths, challenges, and triumphs experienced by neurodivergent women. This empowering book celebrates the untapped potential of neurodivergent women and sheds light on the issues they face in a world that often fails to understand or appreciate their perspectives.

Throughout the book, readers will discover inspiring stories of neurodivergent women who have overcome obstacles and achieved remarkable success in various fields. From scientists to artists, entrepreneurs to activists, their journeys serve as a testament to the incredible capabilities and contributions of neurodivergent women.

In addition to personal narratives, the book provides practical advice, strategies, and resources to support neurodivergent women in navigating a society that may not always cater to their unique needs. It addresses the challenges of social interaction, self-advocacy, mental health, and pursuing fulfilling careers, offering actionable insights that empower readers to embrace their neurodivergent identities and thrive.

A force to be reckoned with.

With a captivating writing style that balances informative content with compelling storytelling, Neurodivergent Women: A Force to Be Reckoned With aims to challenge stereotypes, foster understanding, and inspire both neurodivergent women and the broader society to recognize the remarkable force that lies within neurodiversity.

Table of Contents

Overview...2

Introduction 5

Chapter 1 8

Understanding Neurodivergence................................8

Chapter 2..18

The Journey of Neurodivergent Women..................18

Chapter 3 27

Navigating Relationships and Social Interactions.....27

Chapter 4 35

Self-Advocacy and Empowerment 35

Managing Mental Health and Well-being.................44

Chapter 6 51

Thriving in Education and Careers 51

Chapter 7 62

Supportive Resources and Networks 62

Chapter 8 68

The Power of Neurodivergent Women: Success Stories 68

Chapter 9 75

Embracing Neurodiversity: A Call for Change 75

Introduction

As I embark on this journey of sharing my personal experience as a neurodivergent woman, I am filled with both excitement and trepidation. This book is not just a memoir; it is a testament to the power and resilience of neurodivergent women everywhere. It is a celebration of our unique strengths and an exploration of the challenges we face in a world that often fails to understand us.

Neurodivergence, a concept gaining recognition and importance, refers to the natural variations in how our brains are wired. It encompasses conditions such as autism, ADHD, dyslexia, and more. For too long, society has viewed neurodivergent individuals as broken or flawed, but I firmly believe that we are not broken. We are beautifully different, possessing talents and abilities that, when harnessed, can create a force to be reckoned with.

This book seeks to shed light on the untapped potential of neurodivergent women and challenge the misconceptions that surround us. We have stories to share, journeys that have shaped us, and dreams that deserve to be realized. Through the pages of this book, we will celebrate our achievements, navigate the complexities of our existence, and offer guidance to fellow neurodivergent women seeking their paths to success and fulfillment.

In the following chapters, we will delve into various aspects of neurodivergence and its impact on women's lives. We will explore the challenges we face; from the misunderstandings and discrimination we encounter to the social isolation that often engulfs us. Our mental health journeys, intertwined with our neurodivergent identities, will be laid bare, revealing the struggles we endure and the resilience that carries us forward.

But this book is not just a narrative of hardships; it is a beacon of hope. We will showcase the achievements of remarkable neurodivergent women who have defied societal expectations and carved their paths to success. Their stories will inspire us to embrace our unique strengths and find our voices amidst the noise of conformity.

Additionally, this book will serve as a practical guide, offering insights and strategies for navigating a world that is not always designed with our needs in mind. From self-advocacy and building meaningful connections to managing our

A force to be reckoned with.

mental health and pursuing fulfilling careers, we will discover the tools and resources necessary to thrive.

In the pages ahead, we will embark on a transformative journey together. I invite you, dear reader, to join me as we challenge stereotypes, shatter glass ceilings, and unlock the true potential of neurodivergent women. It is my sincerest hope that this book becomes not just a bestseller, but a catalyst for change, fostering a more inclusive and accepting world for all.

Now, let us begin this extraordinary exploration of neurodivergent women's lives, armed with empathy, understanding, and a determination to rewrite the narrative that has confined us for far too long.

Chapter 1

Understanding Neurodivergence

From the moment I realized that I was different, I embarked on a journey of self-discovery. It was a path filled with challenges, but also with triumphs and the realization that being a neurodivergent woman is not a flaw, but a unique and beautiful aspect of who I am. In this chapter, I invite you to join me on this transformative journey as we explore the essence of our neurodivergent identity, defining what it truly means to be neurodivergent and delving into the various conditions that encompass our diverse experiences.

Embracing the Spectrum of Neurodiversity

Neurodivergence is a broad term that encompasses a wide range of conditions, including autism, ADHD, dyslexia, and Tourette syndrome. These conditions can affect our cognitive abilities, social interactions, and sensory processing. However, they also give us unique strengths and perspectives.

Unleashing Neurodivergent Superpowers

A force to be reckoned with.

People with neurodivergent conditions often have amazing strengths and abilities. For example, people with autism may have a heightened attention to detail or an incredible ability to focus. People with ADHD may be highly creative or have boundless energy. And people with dyslexia may have a gift for visual thinking or problem-solving.

Challenging Misconceptions with Warmth and Understanding

There are many misconceptions about neurodivergence. Some people believe that people with neurodivergent conditions are "broken" or "not normal." Others believe that we are incapable of success or happiness. However, these misconceptions are simply not true.

In this section, we will challenge these misconceptions. We will show the world that people with neurodivergent conditions are just as capable of success and happiness as anyone else. We will also show that our differences are not weaknesses, but rather strengths.

Highlighting the unique strengths and challenges associated with neurodivergence

Embracing Our Superpowers

I am a neurodivergent woman, and I am proud of it. I know that I see the world in an I have always known that I was different. I was sensitive to noise and light, and I had trouble with social interactions. I also had difficulty with executive functioning tasks, such as planning and organizing.

As I got older, the challenges of being neurodivergent became more difficult to manage. I struggled in school, and I had trouble making friends. I also felt like I didn't belong anywhere.

But then, something happened. I started to learn more about neurodiversity. I realized that I wasn't broken and that I wasn't alone. There were other people out there who saw the world in the same way that I did.

This realization gave me the power to start to embrace my neurodiversity. I started to focus on my strengths, and I learned how to manage my challenges. I also started to find supportive people who understood me.

A force to be reckoned with.

Of course, I also face certain challenges. I am sensitive to sensory stimuli, and I have difficulty with executive functioning. I also struggle with social interactions at times.

But I have learned to overcome these challenges. I have found ways to manage my sensory sensitivities, and I have developed coping mechanisms for my executive functioning difficulties. I have also learned how to navigate social interactions in a way that works for me.

I know that I am capable of great things. I have a bright mind, and I am passionate about my work. I am also a strong and independent woman, and I am not afraid to stand up for myself.

I am proud to be a neurodivergent woman, and I know that I have the power to make a difference in the world.

Tips for Embracing Your Strengths and Navigating Your Challenges

Neurodivergent women are those who have brains that work differently than the brains of most people. This can lead to a range of challenges, but it can also lead to unique strengths.

In this section, we will discuss some tips for neurodivergent women on how to embrace their strengths and navigate their challenges.

Identify Your Strengths

The first step to embracing your strengths is to identify them. What are you naturally good at? What do you enjoy doing? Once you know your strengths, you can start to focus on developing them further.

For example, if you are good at problem-solving, you could look for opportunities to use your skills in your work or volunteer activities. If you enjoy writing, you could start a blog or write short stories.

Find Supportive People

It is important to surround yourself with people who understand and appreciate your neurodivergent differences. These people can offer you support, encouragement, and advice.

You may find that you connect with other neurodivergent women in online or in-person communities. You could also talk to your friends, family, or therapist about your experiences.

Set Realistic Goals

A force to be reckoned with.

It is important to set realistic goals when you are neurodivergent. This is because neurodivergent women often have to work harder than neurotypical women to achieve their goals. By setting small, achievable goals, neurodivergent women can build their confidence and self-esteem.

For example, if you want to get a job, you could start by volunteering or shadowing someone in your desired field. Once you have some experience, you can start applying for jobs.

Celebrate Your Successes

It is important to celebrate your successes, no matter how small they may seem. This will help you stay motivated and focused on your goals.

Even small successes are worth celebrating. For example, if you were able to complete a task that you found challenging, give yourself a pat on the back.

Understand Your Challenges

The first step to overcoming a challenge is to understand it. What are the triggers that make your challenge worse? What coping mechanisms can you use to manage your challenge?

For example, if you have difficulty with social interactions, you could learn about social cues and how to read body language. You could also practice social skills in low-pressure situations, such as talking to a cashier or making small talk with a coworker.

Ask for Help

There is no shame in asking for help. In fact, it is a sign of strength. By asking for help, you are acknowledging that you need support, and you are taking steps to improve your situation.

You may want to talk to a therapist, counselor, or other mental health professional. You could also join a support group or connect with other neurodivergent women online.

Take Care of Yourself

It is important to take care of yourself physically and mentally. This includes getting enough sleep, eating healthy foods, and exercising regularly. By taking care of yourself, you will be better able to cope with your challenges and thrive.

A force to be reckoned with.

Breaking Down Misconceptions and Stereotypes

There are many misconceptions and stereotypes about neurodivergent women. These misconceptions can be harmful, as they can lead to discrimination and prejudice.

In this section, we will discuss some of the most common misconceptions about neurodivergent women, and we will provide some information to help break down these misconceptions.

Misconception: Neurodivergent women are "broken."
Fact: Neurodivergent women are simply different, and their differences should be celebrated. Just like neurotypical women, neurodivergent women have a wide range of strengths and abilities.

Misconception: Neurodivergent women cannot be successful.
Fact: Many neurodivergent women are successful in their careers, their relationships, and their lives. Many neurodivergent women have found that

their neurodivergence has given them unique strengths that have helped them to succeed. Misconception: Neurodivergent women are all the same.

Fact: There is a wide range of neurodivergent experiences, and each woman is unique. Neurodivergent women may have different diagnoses, different levels of functioning, and different ways of coping with their challenges.

Embracing Authenticity
It is important to remember that neurodivergent women are not defined by their challenges. They are defined by their unique perspectives, their talents, and their contributions to the world.

We should all embrace our authenticity and celebrate our differences. When we do this, we create a more inclusive and understanding world for everyone.

Additional Tips for Neurodivergent Women
Find your tribe. There are many online and in-person communities for neurodivergent women.

A force to be reckoned with.

These communities can provide you with support, advice, and a sense of belonging.
Don't be afraid to ask for help. If you are struggling with a challenge, don't be afraid to ask for help from a friend, family member, therapist, or other professional.
Take care of yourself. Make sure you are getting enough sleep, eating healthy foods, and exercising regularly. Taking care of your physical and mental health will help you cope with your challenges.

Chapter 2.

The Journey of Neurodivergent Women

The stories of neurodivergent women are often untold. This is because neurodivergence is often misunderstood, and neurodivergent women may feel like they have to hide their differences to fit in.

However, many neurodivergent women are speaking out about their experiences. They are sharing their stories to raise awareness of neurodivergence and to help other neurodivergent women feel less alone.

In this chapter, we will share some personal stories of neurodivergent women from diverse backgrounds. These stories will show that neurodivergence is not a barrier to success. Neurodivergence can be a source of strength and creativity.

Ashley's Story

Ashley is a 25-year-old woman with autism. She was diagnosed with autism when she was two years old. Ashley's parents were told that she would never be able to live independently or hold a job.

A force to be reckoned with.

However, Ashley has defied the odds. She graduated from college with a degree in computer science, and she now works as a software engineer at a major tech company. Ashley is also a passionate advocate for neurodiversity. She speaks out about her experiences to raise awareness of autism and to help other autistic people feel less alone.

Ashley's story is an inspiration to us all. She shows us that it is possible to achieve great things even if you are neurodivergent. She is a living example of the power of neurodiversity.

Sofia's Story

Sofia is a 30-year-old woman with dyslexia. She was diagnosed with dyslexia when she was in the first grade. Sofia struggled in school, and she was often made to feel like she was stupid.

Sofia refused to give up. She worked hard to learn how to read and write, and she eventually graduated from college with a degree in English. Sofia is now a writer, and she is also a mentor to other dyslexic people.

Sofia's story is a testament to the power of perseverance. She shows us that it is possible to overcome any challenge if you are willing to work hard. She is an inspiration to all of us who have ever felt like we were not good enough.

Aisha's Story

Aisha is a 40-year-old woman with ADHD. She was diagnosed with ADHD when she was in the third grade. Aisha struggled in school, and she was often bullied for being different.

Aisha eventually found ways to manage her ADHD. She learned how to focus her attention, and she developed coping mechanisms for dealing with her hyperactivity. Aisha is now a therapist, and she helps other people with ADHD to live successful lives.

Aisha's story is a reminder that neurodivergence is not a disability. It is simply a different way of thinking and processing information. Aisha shows us that it is possible to live a successful and fulfilling life even if you have ADHD.

The Power of Personal Stories

Personal stories are powerful. They can help us to understand the experiences of others, and they can give us hope. The stories of Ashley, Sofia, and Aisha are all inspiring stories of resilience and triumph. They show us that neurodivergence is not a barrier to success.

A force to be reckoned with.

If you are a neurodivergent woman, I encourage you to share your story. Your story could inspire others and help them to feel less alone. You could also use your story to raise awareness of neurodivergence and to advocate for change.

Together, we can create a more inclusive and understanding world for neurodivergent women.

The Power of Vulnerability

In addition to the power of personal stories, the stories of Ashley, Sofia, and Aisha also demonstrate the power of vulnerability. These women were all willing to share their stories, even though they knew that they would be exposing themselves to judgment and criticism.

However, they also knew that their stories could help others, and they were willing to take that risk. This is an important lesson for all of us. We need to be willing to be vulnerable to connect with others and make a difference in the world.

They also knew that their stories could inspire and empower others. By being vulnerable and sharing their struggles and triumphs, they opened the door for others to connect, relate, and find strength in their neurodivergent journeys.

The power of vulnerability lies in its ability to break down barriers and foster understanding. When we share our experiences openly and honestly, we invite others to see us beyond the labels and stereotypes. We create an opportunity for empathy and compassion to flourish, bridging the gap between neurodivergent individuals and the wider society.

Vulnerability is not a sign of weakness but a testament to courage and resilience. It takes strength to reveal our innermost thoughts and emotions, knowing that we may face judgment or rejection. But in doing so, we give voice to the silent struggles, the unspoken fears, and the hidden victories that unite us as neurodivergent women.

Sharing our vulnerabilities can also be a catalyst for change. When we expose the gaps in understanding, challenge misconceptions, and advocate for inclusivity, we contribute to a shift in societal attitudes and systems. By inviting dialogue and education, we can create spaces where neurodivergent women are embraced, supported, and given equal opportunities.

A force to be reckoned with.

As we explore these narratives, I hope that you, dear reader, will recognize the power of vulnerability within yourself. Whether you are a neurodivergent woman, a family member, a friend, or an ally, your vulnerability has the potential to create ripples of change in the lives of those around you. By embracing and sharing your story, you contribute to a more inclusive and compassionate world.

Together, let us celebrate the power of vulnerability and honor the journeys of neurodivergent women. Let us create a society that values and uplifts the unique strengths and perspectives of all individuals, regardless of neurodivergence. By sharing our vulnerabilities, we become catalysts for change, shaping a future where neurodivergent women can thrive and shine.

Now, let us continue this extraordinary exploration of neurodivergent women's lives, armed with empathy, understanding, and a determination to rewrite the narrative that has confined us for far too long.

Exploring the challenges faced in education, employment, and social settings

Neurodivergent women face several challenges in education, employment, and social settings. These challenges can be both external and internal.

External Challenges

Misunderstanding and discrimination. Neurodivergent women often face misunderstanding and discrimination from others. This can make it difficult for them to succeed in school, get a job, or make friends. For example, a neurodivergent woman might be accused of being "lazy" or "unmotivated" because she struggles to focus in class or complete assignments. Or, she might be treated differently by her peers because she doesn't "fit in" with the neurotypical crowd.

Inadequate accommodations. Schools and workplaces often do not provide adequate accommodations for neurodivergent women. This can make it difficult for them to participate fully in these settings. For example, a neurodivergent woman might need extra time on tests or assignments, or she might need a quiet place to work. However, if these accommodations are not provided, she might struggle to keep up with her peers or succeed in her job.

Lack of representation. Neurodivergent women are often underrepresented in schools, workplaces, and social settings. This can make it difficult for them to find role models and mentors. For example, a neurodivergent woman might not see anyone who looks like her or shares her experiences in her textbooks, her workplace, or her social circle. This can make her feel isolated and alone.

Internal Challenges

Sensory overload. Many neurodivergent women are sensitive to sensory input. This can make it difficult for them to focus on school or work, or to participate in social activities. For example, a neurodivergent woman might be overwhelmed by loud noises, bright lights, or crowds. This can make it difficult for her to pay attention in class or to interact with others.

Social anxiety. Many neurodivergent women experience social anxiety. This can make it difficult for them to make friends or to participate in social activities. For example, a neurodivergent woman might worry about saying the wrong thing or making a mistake. This can make her avoid social situations altogether.

Executive dysfunction. Many neurodivergent women have difficulty with executive functioning skills, such as planning, organizing, and time management. This can make it difficult for them to succeed in school or work. For example, a neurodivergent woman might have trouble staying on task or meeting deadlines. This can lead to frustration and discouragement.

Resilience, Self-Discovery, and Personal Growth

Despite these challenges, many neurodivergent women are resilient and go on to achieve great things. They often find ways to overcome their challenges and thrive in education, employment, and social settings.

The key to success for neurodivergent women is often self-discovery and personal growth. By understanding their strengths and weaknesses, and by developing coping mechanisms for their challenges, neurodivergent women can learn to thrive in a world that is not always designed for them.

Chapter 3

Navigating Relationships and Social Interactions

Understanding Social Dynamics and Communication Challenges for Neurodivergent Women

As a neurodivergent woman, I have always found social dynamics and communication to be challenging. I often struggle to understand the unspoken rules of social interaction, and I can find it difficult to express myself in ways that are clear and concise. This can lead to misunderstandings, isolation, and even bullying.

One of the biggest challenges I face is understanding nonverbal communication. I often miss facial expressions, body language, and other cues that neurotypical people use to communicate. This can make it difficult for me to know how someone is feeling or what they are thinking. For example, I might not realize that someone is upset with me until they explicitly tell me.

Another challenge I face is expressing myself clearly and concisely. I often have difficulty finding the right words to say, and I can sometimes come across as blunt or rude. This is because I am not always aware of the impact my words might have on others. For example, I might say something that is meant to be helpful, but it comes across as critical or judgmental.

These challenges can make it difficult for me to navigate social situations. I often feel like I am on the outside looking in, and I can sometimes feel like I don't belong. However, I have learned that there are ways to overcome these challenges.

One way I have learned to overcome these challenges is to be more mindful of my social interactions. I try to pay attention to nonverbal communication, and I ask clarifying questions when I am not sure what someone is saying. I also try to be more aware of the impact my words might have on others, and I am careful to choose my words carefully.

Another way I have learned to overcome these challenges is to find supportive people who understand me. I have found that it is helpful to surround myself with people who are patient and understanding, and who are willing to help me navigate social situations.

I know that I am not alone in facing these challenges. Many other neurodivergent women struggle with social dynamics and communication. However, I also know that it is possible to overcome these challenges. With time and effort, we can learn to navigate social situations and communicate effectively.

Tips for Neurodivergent Women

Here are some tips for neurodivergent women who are struggling with social dynamics and communication:

Be mindful of your social interactions. Pay attention to nonverbal communication, and ask clarifying questions when you are not sure what someone is saying.

Be aware of the impact your words might have on others. Choose your words carefully, and be mindful of how they might be interpreted.

Find supportive people who understand you. Surround yourself with people who are patient and understanding, and who are willing to help you navigate social situations.

Don't be afraid to ask for help. If you are struggling, don't be afraid to ask for help from a friend, family member, therapist, or other professional.

Providing Practical Tips for Building and Maintaining Relationships

As a neurodivergent woman, I know that building and maintaining relationships can be challenging. I often struggle to understand the unspoken rules of social interaction, and I can find it difficult to express myself in ways that are clear and concise. This can lead to misunderstandings, isolation, and even bullying.

However, I have also learned that it is possible to build and maintain meaningful relationships, even if you are neurodivergent. Here are some practical tips that have helped me:

Be yourself. Don't try to be someone you're not. People will appreciate you for who you are, neurodivergent quirks, and all.

Find your tribe. There are other neurodivergent women out there who understand what you're going through. Find them and build relationships with them.

A force to be reckoned with.

Be patient. It takes time to build and maintain relationships. Don't get discouraged if it doesn't happen overnight.

Be honest. If you're struggling with something, be honest with your friends and family. They can help you through it.

Ask for help. If you're feeling overwhelmed, don't be afraid to ask for help from a friend, family member, therapist, or other professional.

Building and maintaining relationships is an important part of life. It can be challenging for neurodivergent women, but it is possible. With time, effort, and patience, you can build strong and meaningful relationships.

Here are some additional tips that may be helpful for neurodivergent women who are building and maintaining relationships:

Be mindful of your communication style. Neurodivergent women often have different communication styles than neurotypical women. Be mindful of how you communicate with others, and be clear and concise in your language.

Be open to feedback. Ask your friends and family for feedback on your communication style. This can help you identify areas where you can improve.

Find common ground. Find things that you have in common with others. This can help you build rapport and connect with others on a deeper level.

Be yourself. Don't try to be someone you're not. People will appreciate you for who you are, neurodivergent quirks, and all.

Remember, you are not alone. There are many other neurodivergent women out there who are building and maintaining meaningful relationships. With time, effort, and patience, you can too.

Addressing Issues Related to Social Anxiety,

Loneliness, and Social Inclusion

As a neurodivergent woman, I know that social anxiety, loneliness, and social exclusion are all common challenges that we face. These challenges can have a significant impact on our mental health, well-being, and ability to participate fully in society.

- Social anxiety is a type of anxiety disorder that is characterized by fear and avoidance of social situations. People with social anxiety often worry about being judged or evaluated by others, and they may experience physical symptoms such as sweating, blushing, or nausea in social situations.

- Loneliness is a subjective experience of social isolation. People who feel lonely may feel like they don't have enough meaningful social connections, or they may feel like they are not accepted or valued by others.
- Social exclusion is the experience of being excluded from social groups or activities. People who feel excluded may feel like they don't belong, or they may feel like they are not valued by others.

These challenges can be difficult to overcome,

but some things can be done to address them.

Here are some tips that I have found helpful:

- Identify your triggers. What are the things that make you feel anxious, lonely, or excluded? Once you know your triggers, you can start to develop strategies for coping with them.
- Build your social support network. Surround yourself with people who understand and

support you. These people can help you feel less alone and more connected.

- Get involved in activities you enjoy. This is a great way to meet new people and make friends.
- Seek professional help. If you are struggling to cope with social anxiety, loneliness, or social exclusion, consider seeking professional help. A therapist can help you develop coping strategies and build your social skills.

Chapter 4

Self-Advocacy and Empowerment

As a neurodivergent woman, I know firsthand the importance of recognizing and embracing my strengths and limitations. I have learned that my strengths, such as my attention to detail, my creativity, and my ability to see patterns, can be incredibly valuable assets. However, I have also learned that my limitations, such as my social anxiety and my difficulty with executive functioning, can sometimes make things challenging.

Over the years, I have come to realize that the key to success for neurodivergent women is to find ways to leverage our strengths while also finding strategies to overcome our limitations. This is not always easy, but it is possible. By understanding ourselves and our unique needs, we can create a life that is both fulfilling and manageable.

In this chapter, I will explore the diverse range of talents, abilities, and challenges that neurodivergent women possess. I will share personal stories and insights that highlight the power of embracing neurodiversity and finding strategies to overcome challenges. I will also discuss the importance of self-acceptance and resilience, and I will offer tips for creating a supportive and inclusive environment for neurodivergent women.

Unveiling Neurodivergent Strengths

Neurodivergent women often possess exceptional strengths and talents that set them apart. For example, many neurodivergent women are highly gifted in areas such as math, science, and technology. They may also be highly creative and have a unique ability to see patterns and solve problems. In addition, neurodivergent women often have a strong sense of empathy and compassion, and they may be natural leaders.

Navigating Limitations and Challenges

While neurodivergent women have unique strengths, they also face specific challenges that can impact their daily lives. Some common challenges include executive functioning difficulties, sensory sensitivities, social anxiety, and communication barriers. These challenges can make it difficult for neurodivergent women to succeed in school, work, and relationships.

A force to be reckoned with.

Embracing Self-Acceptance and Growth

Recognizing and embracing individual strengths and limitations is a journey of self-discovery and self-acceptance. It is important to remember that everyone is different, and there is no one right way to be neurodivergent. The important thing is to find what works for you and embrace your own unique identity.

Developing self-awareness and self-acceptance

Unveiling the Layers: Exploring Neurodivergent Identities

The first step on the journey to self-awareness is to understand our neurodivergent identities. This means exploring the various facets of our identities, such as our sensory processing differences, cognitive patterns, and social communication styles. It also means understanding how our neurodivergent traits impact our lives, both positively and negatively.

I have found that it can be helpful to journal about my experiences as a neurodivergent woman. This helps me to reflect on my thoughts, feelings, and behaviors, and to identify patterns. I also find it helpful to talk to other neurodivergent women about their experiences. This helps me to feel less alone and to learn from others.

The Power of Self-Awareness: Embracing Strengths and Challenges

Once we have a better understanding of our neurodivergent identities, we can start to develop self-awareness. Self-awareness is the ability to understand our thoughts, feelings, and behaviors. It is also the ability to understand our strengths and weaknesses and to recognize our triggers.

Self-awareness is a powerful tool for navigating our neurodivergent journeys. It helps us to make informed decisions, set realistic goals, and establish effective strategies to overcome challenges. It also helps us to build stronger relationships and to feel more confident and empowered.

Embracing Authenticity: Nurturing Self-Acceptance

Self-acceptance is the fundamental aspect of embracing our neurodivergent identities. It means accepting ourselves for who we are, with our strengths and weaknesses. It also means celebrating our unique qualities and challenging societal expectations and stereotypes.

Self-acceptance is not always easy. We may have been conditioned to believe that there is something wrong with us because we are neurodivergent. However, it is important to remember that there is nothing wrong with us. We are simply different, and that is okay.

Empowering Growth: Personal Development and Goal Setting

Self-awareness and self-acceptance lay the foundation for personal growth and empowerment. When we understand ourselves and accept ourselves, we are free to pursue our dreams and goals. We can set meaningful goals, identify our passions and interests, and develop strategies to achieve them.

We can also advocate for ourselves and seek out opportunities for personal development. We can cultivate resilience in the face of challenges, and we can build a strong support network of people who accept and support us.

Empowering neurodivergent women to assert their needs, set boundaries, and advocate for themselves Understanding Self-Advocacy: The Power of Speaking Up

As a neurodivergent woman, I have personally experienced the strength and effectiveness of advocating for oneself. I have faced many challenges in my life, and I have had to learn how to speak up for myself to get my needs met.

Self-advocacy is the act of speaking up for one's rights, needs, and interests. It is a powerful tool that can help us to achieve our goals, build stronger relationships, and live more fulfilling lives.

However, self-advocacy can be difficult for neurodivergent women. We may be hesitant to speak up because we are afraid of being judged or misunderstood. We may also have difficulty communicating our needs clearly and assertively.

Despite these challenges, self-advocacy is essential for neurodivergent women. When we advocate for ourselves, we are taking control of our lives and demanding to be treated with respect. We are also sending a message to the world that we are capable and worthy of being heard.

Asserting Needs: Communicating Effectively

Effective communication is a vital aspect of self-advocacy. It is important to be able to clearly and assertively express our needs, wants, and boundaries. We also need to be able to listen actively and respectfully to the needs of others.

There are a few key strategies that can help us to communicate effectively. First, we need to be clear about what we want. What are our specific needs and wants? What are our boundaries? Once we know what we want, we need to be assertive in expressing it. This means being direct and confident, but not aggressive. We also need to be respectful of the other person's feelings and boundaries.

Another important communication strategy is active listening. This means paying attention to what the other person is saying, both verbally and nonverbally. It also means paraphrasing what the other person has said to ensure that we have understood them correctly.

By using these communication strategies, we can effectively assert our needs and advocate for ourselves.

Setting Boundaries: Prioritizing Self-Care and Well-being

Setting boundaries is another essential aspect of self-advocacy. Boundaries help us to protect our energy and time, and they allow us to feel comfortable in our skin.

There are a few key things to keep in mind when setting boundaries. First, we need to be clear about what we are willing and not willing to do. We also need to be assertive in communicating our boundaries. Finally, we need to be willing to enforce our boundaries. This means saying no when we need to and walking away from situations that are not healthy for us.

By setting boundaries, we can prioritize our self-care and well-being. We can also create a more positive and fulfilling life for ourselves.

Advocating for Change: Creating Inclusive Environments

Advocacy is not just about asserting our own needs. It is also about creating a more inclusive world for all neurodivergent women. We can do

A force to be reckoned with.

this by raising awareness about neurodiversity, challenging societal norms, and working collaboratively to dismantle barriers.

One way to raise awareness about neurodiversity is to share our stories and experiences. We can also educate others about the challenges and strengths of neurodivergent people. By raising awareness, we can help to break down stereotypes and create a more accepting world.

We can also challenge societal norms by speaking up when we see discrimination or prejudice. We can also work to create more inclusive policies and practices in our schools, workplaces, and communities. By challenging societal norms, we can create a world where all neurodivergent women are treated with respect and dignity.

Chapter 5

Managing Mental Health and Well-being

Managing mental health is a challenge for everyone, but it can be especially difficult for neurodivergent women. This is because neurodivergent women are more likely to experience mental health challenges than their neurotypical peers. There are several factors that contribute to this, including social isolation, discrimination, and challenging sensory environments.

Despite these challenges, neurodivergent women also have a number of strengths that can help them to manage their mental health. These strengths include resilience, unique perspective, and creativity. By understanding these strengths and challenges, neurodivergent women can develop effective coping mechanisms and live healthy and fulfilling lives.

Understanding the Mental Health Landscape for

Neurodivergent Women

Neurodivergent women are more likely to experience mental health challenges than their neurotypical peers. This is due to a number of factors, including:

Social isolation: Neurodivergent women may feel isolated from their peers and society as a whole. This can lead to feelings of loneliness, anxiety, and depression.

Discrimination: Neurodivergent women may experience discrimination in school, the workplace, and other areas of life. This can lead to feelings of shame, anger, and resentment.

Challenging sensory environments: Neurodivergent women may be sensitive to noise, light, touch, and other sensory stimuli. This can make it difficult to focus, learn, and function in everyday life.

Communication difficulties: Neurodivergent women may have difficulty communicating their thoughts and feelings. This can lead to misunderstandings, conflict, and social isolation.

Nurturing Inner Strengths: Building Resilience and Coping Strategies

Despite these challenges, neurodivergent women also have a number of strengths that can help them to manage their mental health. These strengths include:

Resilience: Neurodivergent women are often resilient and resourceful. They have learned to adapt to challenges and find creative solutions.

Unique perspective: Neurodivergent women often have a unique perspective on the world. They may see things differently than neurotypical people, which can be a valuable asset.

Creativity: Neurodivergent women are often creative and artistic. They may find that expressing themselves through art, music, or writing is a helpful way to manage their mental health.

Seeking Support: Creating a Supportive Network

One of the most important things that neurodivergent women can do to manage their mental health is to seek support. This support can come from a variety of sources, including:

Professional therapy: Therapy can help neurodivergent women to understand their mental health challenges and develop coping mechanisms.

Peer support groups: Peer support groups can provide a safe space for neurodivergent women to connect with others who understand their experiences.

A force to be reckoned with.

Online communities: There are several online communities for neurodivergent women. These communities can provide support, resources, and a sense of community.

 Practicing Self-Care: Holistic Approaches to Well-being

Self-care is also essential for managing mental health. This includes taking care of your physical, emotional, and spiritual well-being. Some self-care practices that can be helpful for neurodivergent women include:

Engaging in regular exercise: Exercise can help to improve mood, reduce stress, and boost self-esteem.

Maintaining healthy routines: Creating and sticking to healthy routines can help to reduce stress and improve overall well-being.

Nurturing creativity: Expressing yourself creatively can be a helpful way to manage stress and connect with your inner self.

Embrace self-acceptance: Neurodivergent women often have a hard time accepting themselves. However, it is important to remember that you are worthy of love and respect, just the way you are.

Advocating for Mental Health: Challenging Stigma and Promoting Accessibility

Finally, neurodivergent women can also help to improve mental health by advocating for themselves and others. This includes challenging stigma, promoting awareness, and advocating for accessible mental health services.

By advocating for mental health, neurodivergent women can help to create a more inclusive and supportive society for everyone.

The challenges of managing stress and anxiety are well-known to neurodivergent women. I have always been sensitive to sensory stimuli, and I often find social interactions overwhelming. This can lead to heightened stress levels and anxiety, which can make it difficult to function in everyday life.

However, I have also learned how to manage my stress and anxiety in a way that allows me to thrive. I have found that there are some strategies that can be helpful for neurodivergent women, including:

Understanding stress and anxiety in the neurodivergent context: It is important to understand the unique challenges that neurodivergent women face in navigating daily stressors and managing anxiety. By recognizing these challenges, we can tailor strategies that address our specific needs.

Developing stress management techniques: Stress management is crucial for maintaining mental well-being. There is a range of effective stress management techniques that can be particularly beneficial for neurodivergent women, such as mindfulness, deep breathing exercises, meditation, physical activity, and time management.

Reducing anxiety and promoting emotional wellness: Anxiety can be a prevalent challenge for neurodivergent women. Many strategies help reduce anxiety promoting emotional wellness, such as cognitive-behavioral therapy (CBT), grounding exercises, journaling, relaxation techniques, and self-compassion practices.

The power of self-care: Nurturing the mind, body, and soul: Self-care is a vital aspect of maintaining overall well-being. There are many different self-care activities that can be helpful for neurodivergent women, such as engaging in hobbies, practicing self-compassion, setting boundaries, prioritizing rest and relaxation, and seeking sensory-friendly experiences.

Accessing mental health support and resources: Accessing appropriate mental health support and resources is essential for neurodivergent women's well-being. There are a number of resources available, such as therapists, counselors, and psychiatrists who are knowledgeable about neurodiversity. There are also community resources, support groups, helplines, and online platforms that can offer guidance and connection.

I have found that these strategies have helped me to manage my stress and anxiety, and they have allowed me to live a more fulfilling life. I encourage other neurodivergent women to explore these strategies and find what works best for them.

Chapter 6

Thriving in Education and Careers

Finding an educational environment that supports the needs of neurodivergent women is essential for their academic success and personal growth. I know this firsthand, as I have always been different from my peers and have often felt like I didn't fit in. This has made it difficult for me to succeed academically. However, I have also learned that there are educational environments that are supportive of neurodiversity. These environments are characterized by inclusivity, understanding, and flexibility. They provide the necessary accommodations and support services that allow neurodivergent students to thrive.

Recognizing the Importance of Inclusive Education

Inclusive education is essential for the academic success and personal growth of neurodivergent women. In an inclusive environment, neurodivergent students are valued and respected for their unique strengths and abilities. They are not made to feel different or excluded.

There are many benefits to learning in an inclusive environment. For example, neurodivergent students in inclusive environments are more likely to feel confident and self-assured. They are also more likely to develop positive relationships with their peers and teachers.

Researching Educational Institutions

The first step in finding a supportive educational environment is to research different schools and institutions. There are a number of factors to consider when researching educational institutions, such as:

The availability of support services: Does the school or institution offer accommodations and support services that meet your needs?

The expertise of faculty and staff: Do the faculty and staff have experience working with neurodivergent students?

The institution's commitment to inclusivity: Is the institution committed to creating a welcoming and inclusive environment for all students?

There are a number of resources available to help you research educational institutions. You can search online, talk to other neurodivergent women, or contact your local disability advocacy organization.

Seeking Accommodations and Support Services

Neurodivergent women often require specific accommodations and support services to thrive in their educational pursuits. These accommodations can vary depending on the individual's needs. However, some common accommodations include:

Extended time on tests: Neurodivergent students may need additional time to complete tests.

A quiet testing environment: Neurodivergent students may need to take tests in a quiet environment.

A scribe: Neurodivergent students may need a scribe to take notes for them.

In order to receive accommodations, you will need to contact the school or institution's disability support office. The disability support office will work with you to determine what accommodations you need and how to implement them.

Building Relationships with Mentors and Allies

Having mentors and allies can significantly contribute to the success of neurodivergent women in educational settings. Mentors can provide guidance, support, and advocacy. Allies can be friends, family members, or peers who can offer understanding and support.

There are a number of ways to build relationships with mentors and allies. You can ask your teachers or professors for recommendations. You can also join support groups or organizations for neurodivergent women.

Developing Self-Advocacy Skills

Self-advocacy is a crucial skill for neurodivergent women to navigate educational environments effectively. Self-advocacy means speaking up for your needs and rights. It also means being assertive and confident.

There are a number of ways to develop self-advocacy skills. You can take a self-advocacy class. You can also read books or articles about self-advocacy.

By developing self-advocacy skills, you can empower yourself to advocate for your needs and rights in educational settings. You can also collaborate with educators and other stakeholders to create a more inclusive and supportive learning environment.

A force to be reckoned with.

guidance and advice for pursuing fulfilling professional paths

Navigating the professional world can be challenging for anyone, but it can be especially challenging for neurodivergent women. We may have different strengths and needs than our neurotypical peers, and we may face discrimination or prejudice in the workplace.

However, it is possible for neurodivergent women to thrive in their careers. With the right strategies and support, we can find fulfilling and rewarding careers that align with our strengths and aspirations.

Self-Assessment and Identifying Strengths

The first step in finding a fulfilling career path is to understand your own strengths and interests. What are you passionate about? What are you good at? What kind of work environment do you thrive in?

There are many different ways to explore your strengths and interests. You can take personality tests, career assessments, or simply reflect on your experiences.

Once you have a good understanding of your strengths and interests, you can start to identify career paths that are a good fit for you. There are many different career paths that are well-suited for neurodivergent women. Some examples include:

Software development: Software developers often have strong analytical and problem-solving skills. They may also be drawn to the creative aspects of software development.

Data analysis: Data analysts use their analytical skills to make sense of large amounts of data. They may also be drawn to the problem-solving aspects of data analysis.

Education: Neurodivergent women may be well-suited for careers in education, as they can often relate to students who are neurodivergent.

Social work: Neurodivergent women may be well-suited for careers in social work, as they can use their empathy and understanding to help others.

Skill-Building and Professional Development

Once you have identified a career path that you are interested in, you can start to develop the skills that you need to be successful. There are many different ways to build skills, such as formal education, vocational training, online courses, and volunteering.

You can also seek mentorship and networking opportunities to develop industry-specific skills and gain valuable insights into desired professions.

Job Search Strategies

Once you have the skills you need, you can start your job search. There are many different ways to find jobs, such as online job boards, networking, and cold calling.

It is important to tailor your job search to your specific skills and interests. You should also be prepared to advocate for yourself and explain why you are a good fit for the job.

Disclosing Neurodivergence in the Workplace

The decision to disclose one's neurodivergence in the workplace is a personal one. There are potential benefits and challenges to disclosure, and it is important to weigh these factors carefully before making a decision.

If you do decide to disclose, it is important to do so in a way that feels comfortable for you. You should also be prepared to educate your employer about neurodiversity and the accommodations that you may need.

Self-Advocacy and Workplace Support

Neurodivergent women can thrive in their careers by developing self-advocacy skills and accessing appropriate workplace support. This includes being able to effectively communicate your needs, set boundaries, and seek accommodations.

It is also important to build relationships with mentors, peers, and employee resource groups who can provide support and advocacy.

Addressing Workplace Accommodations, Disclosure, and Self-Advocacy

Navigating the workplace can be challenging for anyone, but it can be especially challenging for neurodivergent women. We may have different strengths and needs than our neurotypical peers, and we may face discrimination or prejudice in the workplace.

However, it is possible for neurodivergent women to thrive in their careers. With the right strategies and support, we can find fulfilling and rewarding careers that align with our strengths and aspirations.

Understanding Workplace Accommodations

Workplace accommodations are essential to ensure that neurodivergent women have equal opportunities to succeed in their professional endeavors. I have personally benefited from workplace accommodations, such as flexible work hours, a quiet workspace, and assistive technology. These accommodations have allowed me to work effectively and contribute to my team.

There are many different types of workplace accommodations available, and the specific accommodations that you need will depend on your individual needs and circumstances. If you think that you may need accommodations, it is important to talk to your employer and work together to find the accommodations that work best for you.

Disclosure in the Workplace

The decision to disclose one's neurodivergence in the workplace is a personal one. There are potential benefits and challenges to disclosure, and it is important to weigh these factors carefully before making a decision.

Me, I decided to disclose my neurodivergence to my employer because I felt that it would help me to be more effective in my role. I also felt that it was important for my employer to understand my needs and to be able to provide me with the accommodations that I needed.

If you decide to disclose your neurodivergence, it is important to do so in a way that feels comfortable for you. You should also be prepared to educate your employer about neurodiversity and the accommodations that you may need.

Effective Communication and Self-Advocacy

Developing effective communication skills is crucial for neurodivergent women to advocate for their needs in the workplace. I have found that it is important to be assertive and to be able to clearly communicate my needs and concerns. I have also found that it is helpful to be able to set boundaries and to say no when I need to.

Self-advocacy is also important for neurodivergent women in the workplace. I have learned that it is important to be able to speak up for myself and to advocate for my rights. I have also learned that it is important to be prepared to challenge discrimination and prejudice.

A force to be reckoned with.

Building a Supportive Network

Creating a supportive network is vital for neurodivergent women in their professional lives. I have found that it is helpful to have mentors, colleagues, and friends who understand my neurodivergence and who can provide support and guidance. I have also found that it is helpful to be involved in professional organizations and networks that cater to neurodivergent individuals.

Navigating Career Advancement

Neurodivergent women have the potential to achieve career advancement and pursue leadership roles. I believe that it is important for neurodivergent women to set career goals and pursue opportunities for growth and development. I have also found that it is important to build a strong professional reputation and to network with others.

Chapter 7

Supportive Resources and Networks

Finding supportive resources and networks is essential for neurodivergent women to thrive in their personal and professional lives. These resources can provide a sense of belonging, empowerment, and guidance.

Organizations

There are many organizations that focus specifically on supporting and advocating for neurodivergent women. These organizations work to raise awareness, provide resources, and create inclusive spaces for neurodivergent women to thrive.

Online Communities and Forums

The internet has provided a platform for neurodivergent women to connect, share experiences, and seek support from others who understand their unique journeys. There are many online communities and forums that are specifically designed for neurodivergent women. These platforms allow for open discussions, resource-sharing, and the opportunity to connect with individuals facing similar challenges.

Social Media Groups

Social media platforms have become important spaces for neurodivergent women to find supportive communities. There are many social media groups that focus on neurodivergent women's experiences, challenges, and achievements. These groups offer a space for neurodivergent women to connect, share stories, seek advice, and celebrate their successes.

Mentorship Programs

Mentorship programs tailored to neurodivergent women can provide valuable guidance, support, and professional development opportunities. There are many mentorship programs that specifically focus on empowering neurodivergent women in their educational and professional journeys.

Tips for Finding Support

Start by looking for resources that are led by neurodivergent women themselves. These resources are more likely to understand the unique challenges and experiences of neurodivergent women, and they are more likely to provide the kind of support that is truly meaningful.

Search for online communities and forums that are specifically designed for neurodivergent women. These communities can provide a safe and supportive space for you to connect with others who understand your experiences.

Follow neurodivergent women on social media. This is a great way to stay up-to-date on the latest news and resources for neurodivergent women, and it can also help you connect with other neurodivergent women who share your interests.

Consider participating in a mentorship program. Mentorship programs can provide you with valuable guidance and support from someone who has experience navigating the challenges of being a neurodivergent woman.

Resources for healthcare, therapy, and

specialized services

I understand the importance of accessing the right healthcare, therapy, and specialized services that cater to the unique needs of neurodivergent women. These resources play a crucial role in managing our mental health, addressing specific challenges, and promoting overall well-being.

A force to be reckoned with.

Moreover, I recognize the power of building support networks and fostering a sense of community, as they provide a strong foundation for our journey of self-discovery and empowerment.

Healthcare Providers

When it comes to healthcare, finding providers who genuinely understand our neurodivergent experiences is vital. I have found that it is important to find healthcare providers who are willing to listen to my experiences and who are open to learning about neurodivergence. I have also found that it is helpful to find healthcare providers who are patient and understanding, as I may need to explain things in a different way or ask for clarification.

Therapists and Counselors

Therapy and counseling are incredibly valuable for neurodivergent women, but it's crucial to find professionals who are knowledgeable and experienced in working with individuals like us. I have found that therapy has been a valuable resource for me in managing my mental health and addressing my specific challenges. My therapist has helped me to understand my neurodivergence, develop coping strategies, and build self-esteem. She has also been a source of support and guidance as I navigate the challenges of being a neurodivergent woman in society.

Specialized Services

Our unique challenges often require specialized services tailored to our needs. I have found that assistive technology has been a valuable resource for me in managing my challenges. I use a communication device to help me communicate with others, and I use apps to help me with tasks such as planning and organizing. Assistive technology has made it possible for me to participate in activities that I would not be able to do otherwise, such as going to school and working.

Support Networks and Communities

Building support networks and finding communities where we can be ourselves is crucial. These connections provide spaces where we can share experiences, seek advice, and find understanding from others who have similar journeys. I have found that it is helpful to connect with other neurodivergent women who share my

A force to be reckoned with.

experiences. I have found support groups, online communities, and social media groups to be valuable resources. These groups have provided me with a sense of community and a place to share my experiences with others who understand.

Chapter 8

The Power of Neurodivergent Women: Success Stories

I am inspired by the countless stories of neurodivergent women who have achieved success in various fields. These women have faced challenges and obstacles, but they have never given up on their dreams. They have embraced their neurodivergent identities and used their unique strengths to make a significant impact on the world.

The STEM Trailblazer

One of my favorite neurodivergent success stories is that of Dr. Sarah Martinez. Dr. Martinez is a brilliant neuroscientist who has made groundbreaking discoveries in the field of autism spectrum disorder (ASD). She was diagnosed with ASD at a young age, and she faced numerous challenges in traditional educational settings. However, her passion for understanding the complexities of the human brain drove her to pursue a career in science.

A force to be reckoned with.

Today, Dr. Martinez is a leading researcher in the field of ASD. She is the director of a renowned research institute that is dedicated to finding new treatments and interventions for ASD. Dr. Martinez is also a strong advocate for neurodiversity. She believes that people with ASD have unique gifts and talents that can be used to benefit society.

The Creative Visionary

Another neurodivergent woman who I admire is Jane Thompson. Jane is a talented artist and designer who has revolutionized the world of modern art. She was diagnosed with dyslexia and dysgraphia as a child, and she struggled in conventional learning environments. However, she channeled her energy into her passion for art. Her unique perspective and creative vision have earned her international recognition and awards.

Jane's work often explores the intersection of neurodiversity and creativity. She believes that people with neurodivergent brains often have a unique way of seeing the world, which can lead to innovative and creative solutions. Jane's work is a powerful reminder that neurodiversity is a gift, not a curse.

The Social Entrepreneur

Marie Johnson is a charismatic neurodivergent entrepreneur who founded a successful tech startup that focuses on creating accessible and innovative assistive technologies. Marie was diagnosed with ADHD and dyspraxia as a child, and she experienced firsthand the challenges faced by neurodivergent individuals in the tech industry. Determined to make a difference, she launched her company, providing employment opportunities for other neurodivergent individuals and addressing unmet needs in the assistive technology market.

Marie's company is a shining example of how neurodiversity can be a source of strength and innovation. Her company's products are designed to meet the needs of neurodivergent individuals, and they are helping to make the tech industry more accessible and inclusive.

The Empowering Advocate

Stephanie Carter is a neurodivergent activist who has devoted her life to advocating for the rights and well-being of neurodivergent individuals. Stephanie was diagnosed with ADHD and autism as a child, and she experienced discrimination and prejudice throughout her life. Refusing to be silenced, she became a passionate advocate for

A force to be reckoned with.

neurodiversity acceptance and education. Her impactful TED talks and writings have sparked important conversations on the value of neurodivergent perspectives in society.

Stephanie's work is helping to change the way that society views neurodiversity. She is showing the world that people with neurodivergent brains are not broken, but rather they have unique gifts and talents that can be used to benefit society.

The Trailblazing Athlete

Mia Williams is a talented neurodivergent athlete who has defied the odds in the world of sports. Mia was diagnosed with ADHD and dyslexia as a child, and she encountered challenges in traditional educational settings. However, her exceptional athleticism and unwavering determination led her to become an Olympic gold medalist in track and field. Mia uses her platform to raise awareness about neurodiversity in sports and inspire young athletes to pursue their dreams unapologetically.

Mia's story is a powerful reminder that neurodivergent individuals can excel in any field they choose. She is a role model for young people everywhere, showing them that they can achieve anything they set their minds to.

Their Contributions, Innovations, And Impact

As a neurodivergent woman myself, I am inspired by the remarkable contributions, innovations, and impact made by neurodivergent women across various fields. These extraordinary individuals have not only achieved personal success but have also left a lasting imprint on their industries and communities. By exploring their groundbreaking work, we gain a deeper appreciation for the unique perspectives and talents that neurodivergent women bring to the table.

I am particularly interested in the work of neurodivergent women in the field of science. Neurodivergent individuals often have a unique way of thinking and seeing the world, which can lead to new and innovative insights. For example, Dr. Emily Chen, a neurodivergent geneticist, has made groundbreaking discoveries about the genetic basis of neurodevelopmental disorders. Her work has the potential to revolutionize the way we understand and treat these conditions.

I am also inspired by the work of neurodivergent women in the field of technology. Neurodivergent individuals often have a deep understanding of complex systems and a knack for finding creative solutions to problems. For example, Sarah Patel, a neurodivergent computer scientist, has made significant contributions to the field of artificial intelligence. Her work has helped to make AI systems more accurate and efficient, and it has the potential to benefit people of all abilities.

The work of neurodivergent women in these and other fields is a testament to the power of neurodiversity. When we embrace our unique strengths and perspectives, we can make a real difference in the world. I am excited to see what the future holds for neurodivergent women, and I am confident that they will continue to make groundbreaking contributions to society.

Personal Reflections

As a neurodivergent woman, I have faced my fair share of challenges. I have been told that I am "too different" or "not good enough." But I have also been told that I am "brilliant" and "creative." I have learned to embrace my neurodiversity and use my unique strengths to my advantage.

I am grateful for the work of neurodivergent women who have come before me. They have paved the way for me to achieve my dreams. I am confident that the future is bright for

Neurodivergent women

neurodivergent women, and I am excited to see what we will accomplish together.

Chapter 9

Embracing Neurodiversity: A Call for Change

I am a neurodivergent woman. I have been diagnosed with autism spectrum disorder (ASD), and I also have ADHD. These conditions have shaped my life in many ways, both positive and negative.

On the one hand, my neurodiversity has given me a unique perspective on the world. I see things differently than most people, and I often have insights that others don't. I am also very creative and intuitive.

On the other hand, my neurodiversity has also made things difficult for me at times. I have struggled in school and in the workplace. I have also experienced social isolation and discrimination.

But I have learned to embrace my neurodiversity. I have learned to use my strengths to my advantage, and I have found ways to manage my challenges. I am now a successful businesswoman, and I am using my platform to advocate for neurodiversity acceptance.

I believe that neurodiversity is a gift. It gives us a unique perspective on the world, and it allows us to see things in new and innovative ways. We are valuable members of society, and we deserve to be accepted and respected.

Advocating for Greater Acceptance

One of the most important things we can do is to advocate for greater acceptance of neurodivergent women. This means challenging stereotypes and misconceptions about neurodiversity, and working to create more inclusive and supportive environments.

We can challenge stereotypes by sharing our stories and by educating others about neurodiversity. We can also work to create more inclusive environments by advocating for changes in policies and practices.

For example, we can advocate for inclusive educational environments that provide accommodations for neurodivergent students. We can also advocate for inclusive workplaces that offer reasonable accommodations to neurodivergent employees.

Promoting Inclusivity and Understanding

A force to be reckoned with.

We also need to promote inclusivity and understanding in our communities, workplaces, and educational institutions. We need to create environments that embrace diverse ways of thinking, communicating, and interacting.

This means being mindful of our language and behavior and avoiding making assumptions about neurodivergent individuals. It also means being open to learning about neurodiversity and being willing to listen to the experiences of neurodivergent individuals.

Dismantling Societal Barriers

Neurodivergent women face a number of systemic barriers, including limited access to resources, employment discrimination, and inadequate healthcare support. We need to dismantle these barriers through policy changes, workplace accommodations, and increased funding for research and support services.

For example, we can advocate for policies that provide financial assistance to neurodivergent individuals who need it. We can also advocate for changes in the law that would make it illegal to discriminate against neurodivergent individuals in employment.

Promoting Equity

We need to promote equity by providing equal opportunities and resources for neurodivergent women. This includes fair and inclusive hiring practices, educational accommodations, and access to healthcare services.

We can also promote equity by ensuring that neurodivergent women are represented in decision-making positions. This will help to ensure that the needs of neurodivergent individuals are taken into account when policies and practices are being developed.

Actionable Steps for Support

There are a number of actionable steps that individuals, communities, and institutions can take to support neurodivergent women. This includes:

Fostering inclusive and accessible educational environments

Creating supportive workplaces with reasonable accommodations

Offering mental health resources tailored to the specific needs of neurodivergent individuals

A force to be reckoned with.

Building networks and communities where neurodivergent women can connect, share experiences, and find support

Embracing neurodiversity is not only a moral imperative but also an opportunity to tap into the unique talents and perspectives of neurodivergent women. By advocating for greater acceptance, inclusivity, and understanding, we can create a world where neurodivergent women are valued, supported, and celebrated for their contributions. Through dismantling societal barriers and promoting equity, we ensure that all individuals have equal opportunities to thrive. By taking actionable steps to support neurodivergent women, we can foster a society that truly embraces and celebrates neurodiversity.

Together, let us commit to creating a world where the potential of every neurodivergent woman can be realized, and where diversity and inclusion are cherished as the cornerstones of progress.

I believe that we can create a more inclusive and accepting world for neurodivergent women. It will take hard work and dedication, but it is possible. I am committed to doing my part, and I hope that you will join me.

Thank you for reading

Neurodivergent women